Dinosaurs Go Green!

A Guide to Protecting Our Planet

Laurie Krasny Brown and Marc Brown

LITTLE, BROWN AND COMPANY
Books for Young Readers
New York   Boston

For Mike and Ann Shilhan,
who take such beautiful care of their place on the planet

Our special thanks to Michelle Brauner, environmental consultant; Carol Cirillo, teacher, Belmont Day School; Dr. Verne Howe, chairwoman, North American Association of Environmental Educators; Ingrid Kavanagh, founder, Children's Alliance for the Protection of the Environment; Doug Smith, exhibitions planner, Boston Museum of Science; and his son, Gregory Smith.

Little, Brown Books for Young Readers

Hachette Book Group
237 Park Avenue, New York, NY 10017
Visit our Web site at www.lb-kids.com

Little, Brown Books for Young Readers is a division of Hachette Book Group, Inc. The Little, Brown name and logo are trademarks of Hachette Book Group, Inc.

First Revised Paperback Edition: April 2009
Originally published as *Dinosaurs to the Rescue!* in hardcover and paperback by Little, Brown and Company in 1992 and 1994.

The book is printed on recycled paper with nontoxic soy inks.

Library of Congress Cataloging-in-Publication Data

Brown, Laurie Krasny.
   Dinosaurs go green! : a guide to protecting our planet /
Laurie Krasny Brown and Marc Brown. – 1st ed.
   p.   cm.
   Summary: Text and illustrations of dinosaur characters introduce the earth's major environmental problems and suggest ways children can help.
   ISBN 978-0-316-04403-5
   1. Environmental protection – Citizen participation – Juvenile literature. [1. Environmental Protection.] I. Brown, Marc Tolon.
II. Title.
TD171.7.B76   1992
333.7'2 – dc20   91-27177
                        10 9 8 7 6 5 4 3 2 1
                                 SC
                     Manufactured in China

Earth is the only home we have!
Every day our planet offers us fresh air, clean water, and fertile land. But these gifts, called natural resources, won't always be here if we waste or spoil them.
There are many ways we can all help protect our planet!

Use Less

Using only as much as you need of the earth's resources is one way to help. By wasting less, you leave more for tomorrow and for others, too.

Water   We couldn't live without it!

We drink it, cook with it, and use it to wash ourselves and other things. All plants and animals need water to grow and stay healthy.

You can help save water — just turn it off!

Turn off the water while brushing your teeth. A gallon is wasted every minute the faucet is on.

Taking a bath can use up 50 gallons of water. That's 800 glasses!

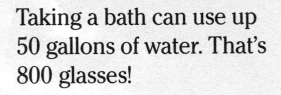
A water-saving showerhead helps use less water, too!

Only run a full dishwasher. Or when you hand-wash dishes, use a basin of soapy water instead of running the tap.

Electricity Every time you or your parents turn something on — lights, heat, the stove, or the car — it uses up energy. You can save energy by turning these things on only when you need them — and turning them off when you are done.

Turn off electric lights and use daylight.

Finished watching TV, listening to the radio, or using the computer? Turn it off!

Opening the refrigerator lets in warm air and wastes electricity. Try to get what you need quickly and then close the door.

Cool off in hot weather by opening windows and curtains at night. Use a fan instead of an air conditioner, which puts harmful gases into the air.

Use your own energy whenever you can.

Cars   The smoke that comes from driving a car pollutes the air by making it dirty and hard to breathe. Share car rides whenever you can, and use other ways to get around.

Paper Trees are natural resources, too. They give us everything from cleaner air, shade, wood, fruit, and nuts to the material for making paper. Trees offer homes for birds and other animals, too.

You can help save trees by using less paper. Use paper up completely before throwing it out or recycling it.

Instead of paper plates and cups, choose dishes and glasses you can wash and use again and again.

Wipe up spills with a reusable sponge or cloth instead of paper towels, which have to be thrown away.

Bring along your own bag or backpack to carry home what you buy at the store.

Plastic Plastic is made from one of the earth's buried resources — oil. If we use up all the oil that's under the ground, there won't be any more!

You can save oil by using less plastic. So many things come wrapped in plastic that just gets thrown away. Take home as little plastic as you can.

Avoid

Single servings

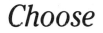

Plastic wrap

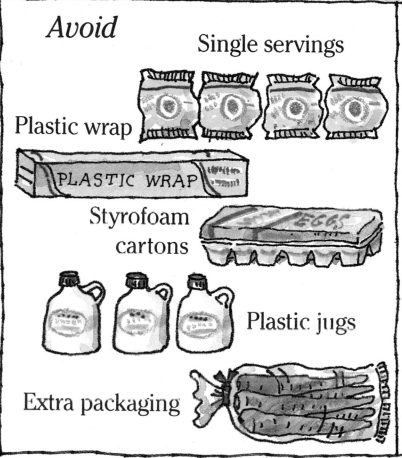

Styrofoam cartons

Plastic jugs

Extra packaging

Choose

Larger packages

Biodegradable waxed paper

Recycled paper cartons

Glass bottles

Less packaging

If you're looking for a snack, try one that doesn't come in plastic but in its own natural package — it's biodegradable.

Use Again

Another way to protect natural resources is to reuse the things you have. Reusing things saves the energy and materials it takes to make new ones. It also pollutes less and leaves less to throw away.

Taking care of toys and supplies helps them last longer.

New Uses

Try finding new uses for things instead of throwing them away.

Turn an old shoe box into a place to keep something special.

Save colorful paper scraps to make cards for your family and friends. Make wrapping paper by decorating newspaper.

Use plastic containers to hold things for picnics or to play with in the tub or at the beach.

You can even make your whole Halloween costume from things you recycle!

Recycling Recycling garbage begins at home. Materials such as glass, metals, and paper can be remade into new recycled products. All you need are boxes or bags for collecting the things your city or town recycles.

New Homes

Finding new homes for things you outgrow allows others to use and enjoy them, too.
You may want to give things away to a hospital or shelter.

Have a family yard sale.

Trade some of your old toys and books with friends or neighbors.

Every time you begin to throw something away, stop and think,
Is there some way I can reuse this?

Give Something Back

The earth keeps us alive. But we can't just take from it all the time. We also need to give something back. You can help by doing all you can to make the outdoors clean and safe.

Throw garbage in litter baskets. Plastic trash can harm animals.

Marking up buildings and walls is a way of trashing them. Help keep them clean.

Cleaning up after your dog makes the streets a nicer and healthier place to be.

Pick up litter wherever you find it!

You can help save the lives of animals and plants. Each one has a reason for being and a unique place in nature.
If you catch an animal or insect, don't keep it. Try to put it back where you found it.

Appreciating plants and animals without taking them home protects nature and leaves them for you and others to enjoy again.

Grow something at home. Every plant helps make the air cleaner and our earth greener.